Testimonials...

"The Road to Innovation is a fast ride for the busy manager or professional looking to get into top gear on this subject. If you want to focus your business on how to kick start innovation and keep it coming, then this is the book for you. Peppered with great examples and questions that make you really think about what innovation means for your organisation, the book is an easy read but one that also repays deeper reflection. Cris has the keys to the innovation highway!"

Peter Cook
MD - Human Dynamics
Author of 'Best Practice Creativity' and 'Sex, Leadership and Rock 'n' Roll'

"The Road to Innovation is a great read for business owners, leaders and managers alike– ridiculously packed with positive ideas and searching questions we've now made it a must read for our team to kick start our thinking and to take a fresh look at how we do things around here."

Nick Bartlett
Director - Zest Learning

"The ability to link theory to practice in order to achieve real world success is an invaluable skill. Cris demonstrates his comprehensive knowledge backed up with real life experiences of delivering innovation in the heat of the business battle. This book will provide much needed help to prepare people in business and the public sector who need to engage with the innovation challenge."

Professor Simon Bolton
Chair of Creative Design - Cranfield University

"The Road to Innovation provides valuable insights and case studies on modern working practices. I like Cris' integrated approach and I noticed some useful tips for growing my own business too!"

Pier Paolo Mucelli
Founder - eOffice

"Cris' street smart style makes this book punchy and straight talking; just the way innovation should be. If you want a quick, simple yet illuminating orientation to what for too long has been perceived as a dark art, look no further."

Chris Barez-Brown

Founder - Upping Your Elvis

Formerly Head of Learning at What If

Author of 'How To Have Kick Ass Ideas'

"I really enjoyed this book and found it to be an interesting and thought-provoking journey. It is the sort of book you want to read again and keep handy so you can "dip into it" as the need arises. I thoroughly recommend it!"

Phil Jesson

Director - The Academy for Chief Executives

"Cris Beswick has finally produced THE field guide on innovation that I'm sure many Organisational Development professionals have been looking for. Under pressure from CEOs, Boards and Senior Executives, this book provides the innovation dots, you join them up and colour them in according to your needs and environment. OD pros need worry no more - for Cris has crafted the roadmap to their innovation El Dorado - and done so without trickery, pretence or mystique. Let's Think Beyond indeed."

Perry Timms

Head of Organisational Development - Big Lottery Fund

The Road to **Innovation...**

Cris Beswick & David Gallagher

Cris Beswick is an accomplished speaker, advisor, author, non-executive director and consultant. Having founded several successful companies over the last decade and following the sale of his last award winning design consultancy, he now works with businesses and organisations to help them understand innovation, helping create the right strategy for it and developing an environment and a community in which it can thrive. The results are great places to work for your people, added value for your customers, and sleepless nights for your competitors.

David Gallagher is a freelance writer who helped Cris dot his i's and cross his t's.

Designed by **www.ltbpublishing.com**

Let's Think Production Co-ordinator - **Nikki O'Sullivan**

Let's Think Graphic Designer - **Gary Nelson**

Cover Photographer - **Louan Hamilton**

First published in 2010 by Let's Think Beyond Ltd

A CIP record for this book is available from the British Library.

ISBN: 978-0-9564858-0-9

Printed and bound in Great Britain by Fingerprint Fo+ Ltd

Contents...

Intro duc tion...

I've entitled this book *The Road to Innovation* because, unlike many of the other thinkers and writers on this subject, I believe that undertaking the journey is far more important – and can be ultimately more beneficial – than reaching an innovation destination.

Your decision to invest your time in reading this book means, I suspect, that one of the key challenges you are facing is how you can build a company or organisation that is successfully founded on a sustainable, entrepreneurial and innovative culture. Innovation is something of a buzz word at the moment, but what does it really mean for you and your business? What do you want innovation to deliver for your business?

Other books you may have read, other people you may have heard speaking or other consultants you may have engaged will I suspect have focused on innovation as a destination – the creation of a brand new product or service that will catapult your business way ahead of your competitors. It is likely they will have drawn evidence from the success of large, multinational companies or dynamic, entrepreneurial start-ups and much of their basic premise lies in the fact that those companies have blazed an innovation trail so all you need to do is replicate what they did and blaze your own.

But... *you and I know it's not that simple!*

I've read sufficient books about the subject that, whilst incredibly detailed and well-researched, at the end of which I still feel they do not offer any practical guidance on how companies, organisations, government or charities can begin their own innovation journey. And as I've already mentioned earlier, starting on the road is far more important than any far off destination. So being able to take what you have read or heard and be able to apply that practically to your own situation from today is crucial and will bring many benefits to your organisation, irrespective of whether you deliver something truly innovative at the end of the journey or not.

Company-wide innovation isn't about creative thinking games or improving brainstorming techniques. I believe it's about your approach to...

Strategy, People, Community Environment, Creativity, Risk and Leadership.

These seven key themes are explored in more detail in each chapter and all play a huge part in getting you, your people and your business further down the road to innovation.

Most business owners and directors I talk to struggle with how to change the way the company operates, how it deals with its people, how it develops and delivers products to its customers.

Innovation is a vehicle that can help make the changes necessary to meet these, and a myriad other, business challenges. I see it as a catalyst that delivers profitable business that is sustainable. Innovation generates creative, entrepreneurial, dynamic and switched on organisations.

I'm sure you've all heard the rallying cry at meetings.

"Guys... we need to be more innovative."

Many people see innovation as doing something unique; doing something for the first time, doing something that changes customer expectations or creates brand new markets. Innovation of course can do all that, but don't put all your energies and focus exclusively to these aims.

My focus for this book is therefore not on doing something truly innovative at the end. The value of thinking more innovatively and of creating the right conditions for innovative ideas to grow, is that the process itself generates many of the changes that businesses want to see – in their people, in their processes, in their products or services.

Innovation is about taking ideas, half-baked notions, competencies, concepts and assets that already exist and reconfiguring them in interesting and different ways that allow new things to emerge. The essence of what is new is the mix, not necessarily the individual components. Think about your own business. Who has full-time responsibility for innovation? It might be you. It might be no one. It might be the research and development department. It might be a small team of senior people drawn from different areas of the business.

But imagine what you could achieve if all employees were constantly thinking differently, constantly coming up with new efficiencies, constantly bringing forward new ideas. There are three things you can start doing today that will help you begin to build up an organisation of this type:

Practice
Practice
Practice

Whether it is the pinnacle of sporting triumph, the solution to a mathematical or scientific challenge or the introduction of a new product or service, success is likely to be the result of endless practice, repetition and refinement, rather than a one-off flash of inspiration or brilliance.

Before we start our journey, let's be clear about what innovation is not.

- Innovation is not the sole domain of high tech industries, the preserve of specialists nor something exclusive to R&D.
- Innovation is not about being first.
- Innovation is not defined by having the highest sales or largest market share.

Here's what I consider to be the truth about innovation.

- Innovation is fuelled by diversity and that means it's about people.
- Most innovations, if you unpack them, are a mix of previously existing ideas.
- Innovation is about the quality of ideas, where the ideas come from, how often and how many ideas you have.

Innovate: \ In"no"vate \ , v.
To begin or introduce something for the first time.

So says the dictionary. But to me this confuses the distinction between innovation, invention and introduction – and in doing so has helped to perpetuate some of the myths around what innovation is. If you begin to do something new in your company that your competitors have been doing for years, is that an innovation? If you invent something that delivers no real value to your customers or your business, is that being innovative? I would answer no in both cases and suggest that the true definition of innovation is this:

Innovate: \ In"no"vate \ , v.
The successful exploitation of an idea that adds value to the customer and commercial return for the creator.

Anything that can be described as an innovation needs to add value. That could be socially, it could change the way a business works so that it becomes more efficient (and therefore more profitable), it could change the way people are managed and motivated (and therefore retain and attract staff, reducing recruitment costs), or it could be a new product or service that helps generate sustainable and profitable business.

The point is this: in order to create something of value to your customer you need to really understand what makes your customer tick. It would be fair to say that most profitable companies are more likely to define themselves as successful, rather than define themselves as a business that is constantly improving and adding value to its customers. But without that strong connection and conversation with customers, that profitability and success is likely to be temporary. It may be months, it may be years, but at some point a competitor will come along who is more engaged and more interested in your customers, or your lack of real understanding means that the market and the customers move on before you do.

Innovation therefore should not be thought of exclusively as doing something new or being the first. It needs to be something that is progressive; an improvement that can be incremental or radical from what already exists. It needs to be something successful; if it's just something different it is an invention, not an innovation. It needs to be something that adds value; for the customer, for the end user, for the creator and, ideally, for all three.

I want to pump some value back into innovation, taking it away from a buzz word or a term over-used and misunderstood that gets people's eyes rolling upwards as opposed to getting them excited. By rigidly sticking to my principles of progressive, successful and adding value, less products and services, companies and organisations may be classed as innovative in the future but those that remain will be far more significant.

If innovation is something you want to work towards, you need to understand what it takes.

- How will you create time and space in people's lives for thinking and experimentation in order for innovation to flourish?
- How will you maximise the diversity of people in your organisation to create the diversity of thinking innovation requires?
- How will you connect different perspectives and viewpoints to generate different takes on what you do and how you do it?

Throughout the book you will see these series of three questions that give you practical starting points to tackle some of the issues and challenges you may need to overcome to get your people and your business in a better position to harness the power of innovation. I'm sure I don't need to remind you of Mark Twain's famous quote, but if you are looking to instil any change in your business you can't do it if you keep doing exactly the same things you always have done. Twain's opinion is still as relevant today as it was in 1910. In fact, it might be even more relevant in terms of highlighting the importance of innovation as an updated version could be along the lines of...

> "What customers want today, they won't want tomorrow."

The 'a-ha!' factor is rare and over-estimated by many people. Some of the most innovative and successful companies in the world, such as Google, Pixar, Nokia, 3M, Dyson and Apple, understand this rarity. Their critical focus is in creating the right community because in doing so, the chances of doing something truly innovative can then multiply exponentially. Under the right conditions an 'a-ha!' moment isn't guaranteed, but it's more likely to happen. Such companies always ensure that their overall business strategy incorporates innovation – in the same way it incorporates financial forecasts, operational management and marketing.

So starting with...

strategy,

I will then explore the other six key elements that I believe are vital on any innovation journey:

People, Community, Environment, Creativity, Risk and Leadership.

I will also provide some practical advice and questions for you to begin to tackle some of these issues in your own organisation.

By addressing and changing these elements in your business, you will deliver an incredibly powerful and positive boost to your organisation. In many cases it will improve your efficiency, your profitability, your retainment of staff, your sales and market share figures. So much so, that I'm confident that even if you don't do something truly innovative as a result of making those changes, your journey on the road to innovation will still have been hugely beneficial to your business.

So, let's start with strategy...

Strat egy...

A question I always ask my clients to help them understand the importance of putting in place a strategy that will create the right conditions for innovation, is this:

Where does quality come from in your organisation?

I think people like that question because it's tangible. They know what quality looks like. They understand it. And most can answer it in detail as well. They've thought long and hard about quality. They may have a quality policy, if large enough a quality manager or team, and they might be one of the almost 900,000 organisations worldwide that use ISO 9001 for their quality framework.[1] Quality, they often tell me, is embedded in their organisation. They invest in training, systems and processes to ensure that a quality approach is maintained by all employees.

So then I say....

Where does innovation come from in your organisation?

And that's when I'm usually met with a bit of a flustered silence.

Modern businesses and organisations invest money, time and resources into tweaking every process and system to the point of perfection. Referring to the earlier question on quality, organisations with a quality approach don't reach a point and say, "Right, that's it, we're now a quality organisation, we can divert resources and efforts to the next problem."

Far from it...

Quality organisations continually measure, review, analyse and adapt their systems and processes to ensure that quality remains consistent at the very worst, and more likely, continues to improve throughout the organisation.

Businesses with efficient supply chains are constantly analysing every thing they do to see if they can do it more efficiently, more cost-effectively and faster. Retailers are constantly reviewing their product lines, their store layouts, their window displays, their pricing to ensure that they keep attracting customers, giving them a good shopping experience and value for money.

So think of the most important process or area in your business, it might be sales, distribution or production – and your strategy for maintaining the focus of everyone in the business on it. Now imagine if you were as unsure about it, as you maybe now are about innovation.

Treat innovation as if it were a business process just like all the others.

- What do you want innovation to achieve for your business?
- Who has overall responsibility for innovation in your organisation?
- Where are you now in terms of innovation and how will you reach your goal?

Most businesses these days want to do 'something innovative'. They, quite rightly, see it as a means of differentiating themselves from the crowded global marketplace. There are plenty of large agencies and expensive innovation consultants who could be brought in to deliver rapid and radical innovation. But the reality for many companies is that such a course of action is simply unaffordable.

What they really want to do is generate sustainable, organic growth through innovation. It is ultimately uneconomical for many organisations to keep buying in expertise. They need to learn to 'fish for themselves'. In order for organisations to do something truly innovative, the principles of innovation need to be clearly understood, the path of innovation clearly defined and the culture of innovation firmly embedded into everything the company does. In short, innovation needs to be part of the organisational DNA.

> **It's easy to come up with new ideas; the hard part is letting go of what worked for you two years ago, but will soon be out of date.**
>
> *Roger van Oech*

It's a simple fact that without creativity and innovation, there will be very few companies in existence today who will still be around in a few years time at a really competitive level. Irrespective of the current economic difficulties as I write this in the summer of 2009, marketplaces are becoming increasingly more competitive and consumers ever more demanding. But whether it's a tough climate or a thriving one, businesses that clearly differentiate their offer or service from their competitors will stay one step ahead of the game.

Innovation is therefore crucial in order to improve business survivability, sustainability and profitability.

"You cannot be remarkable by following someone else who is remarkable."[2]

- Identify your closest three competitors.
- What do you do that is clearly different to them now?
- How will you differentiate from them over the next 2, 3 or 4 years?

Ok, here comes my strategy equation. Whatever your organisation, whatever your business, whether you're an established player or a new start-up, this is fundamentally what should be at the core of your strategy:

INSIGHT + IDEAS = POSSIBILITIES

Many other authors on innovation or consultants you might have talked to would tell you that insight + ideas = innovation. Well, I don't because in the real world, it's just not that simple. If you don't understand what you need to achieve and why; if you don't address people's needs then you're just generating random ideas. By understanding customers and what their problems are, or what they might be in the future, then it's not difficult to come up with ideas.

(And by the way, if you're thinking at this stage that you're not creative, or your people are not creative and they won't be able to come up with ideas, well you're wrong. Thinking creatively can be scary for some people – primarily because it's a change, a break from the norm – but it is a skill that everyone has and can learn to make better use of. And I'll go into creativity in more detail in a separate chapter).

It can be tough for some companies to admit that they don't have good insight into their customers. But it's vital that your strategy is formed from a position of truth. So be brave. Be honest. Because without genuine insight, all the time and effort you and your people put into idea generation, problem solving, developing and creating new products and services (and the subsequent significant investment that requires) could be wasted. You could end up simply generating random ideas, inventing things for the sake of it in the hope that customers buy them.

How well do you know your customers?

- How much information do you have about what your customers think and do now?
- How much analysis do you have on why they do it?
- How could your business satisfy these needs in newer, value added and more competitive ways?

I've worked with enough companies over the years and reviewed a large amount of research to recognise what normally happens when a business decides to innovate. This usually means a period of focused effort and resources on creating and launching new products or services that will boost a plateauing sales performance.

And quite often it works, for a few years.

The problem is that during those years of boosted sales performance, the focus on innovation is lost and the resources diverted elsewhere. So, surprise surprise, a few years later down the line and the company is again faced with a situation where sales have plateaued.

So yes, whilst the business may well have done something innovative and reaped the short-term success, it's innovation founded on sand. It's not organic growth. It's not sustainable. And over the long-term, it's unlikely to be profitable. The normal life cycle of any product can be characterised as...

Innovation ➔ Growth ➔ Maturity (Plateauing) ➔ Decline.

So, a business that doesn't continually innovate and launch new products and services will ultimately decline in proportion as its existing portfolio plateaus.

Even with step change products that revolutionise market sectors, it's vital to be thinking: what's next? When James Dyson launched the first of his bagless vacuum cleaners on the UK market in 1993 he was already working on subsequent models as he knew that, just like every innovation, one day it would become obsolete.

When we've finished developing a machine, we let loose a fresh team of engineers to take it apart, to interrogate each component. How can it work even better? ”

Continual improvement, creative thinking and problem solving is embedded in the company's strategy. Not surprising really, when Dyson's 'overnight' success with the DC01 came after building 5,127 prototypes. And it's a strategy that has at its core one of Dyson's wishes that he shares with all his customers:

I just want things to work properly. ”

Your strategy needs to go beyond competitor benchmarking.

- How can you improve your current top performing product or service?
- Who is going to be given the time, budget and responsibility to drive innovation, creative thinking and change?
- What will your competitors be doing in 5 years time?

Your strategy needs to encourage every person in your organisation to be creative in their approach to all aspects of the business. It needs to promote an environment which has the capacity to lead innovation and give it clear direction and purpose. The strategy needs to be built on relevant and appropriate consumer insight so that you are not simply generating random ideas, but rather using informed creativity to build new products, services or processes that are sustainable and profitable.

In short, it's a strategy that declares being creative and thinking differently is simply part of what we do around here. Companies with innovation at their heart can of course be profitable and successful businesses. Take Logitech for example. Look at the mouse, keyboard, internet headset, speakers, iPod docking station or earphones you use. One or more of them probably displays a Logitech logo.

Logitech sold $2.2billion worth of products in its last financial year.[3] That's pretty impressive, but even more impressive is the fact that it generates more than 50% of its annual revenue from new products. Every year. Logitech recognises that whatever new product it brings out, no matter whether it is more comfortable, more fun, more productive or delivers a richer user experience, it's likely to be taken for granted or obsolete within 12-18 months.

The corporate strategy therefore focuses on ensuring that 50% of its annual revenue comes from new products. Now, you may be an owner, director or manager in a business where products may have a longer life cycle, but it's crucial that your strategy ensures that your new products and services are the ones that make your existing ones obsolete. Because the alternative is that it's your competitors who do that, or you find yourself trying to sell products where there is no longer a customer need.

Either way, you're in big trouble!

“Don’t strive to be considered the best of the best. You want to be considered the only ones who do what you do.”[4]

- Identify the products or services that you want to make obsolete in 12-24 months.
- Using customer insight, what new ideas could you turn into profitable products or services and launch within 12-24 months?
- How would you improve on your competitors’ best selling products or services?

Your strategy should identify which type of innovation you are committed to:

Incremental, Radical, or Revolutionary?

- Incremental: Small, constant steps forward.
- Radical: Usually fast, major leaps forward.
- Revolutionary: When a collection of radical ideas changes things on a massive scale.

The type of innovation you need will depend on a number of factors, including:

- Do you want to take small steps forward?
- Do you need to take major leaps?
- How quickly do you need to move?
- What type of market do you operate in?
- What budget and resource can you allocate?

There is no wrong or right answer. Radical innovation can be undertaken at a fast pace and can lead to revolutionary changes to your market that put you way ahead of your competitors. The downside is it is usually more expensive, you are likely to have to buy in expertise in order to do it and therefore it is unlikely to leave a sustainable, organisational culture of innovation once the external resources have left.

I would argue that most businesses should aim for a strategy of incremental innovation. It is less expensive and less risky. It helps embed a new way of thinking and operating amongst the people in your organisation so that it becomes part of the culture. And ultimately it's a route to revolutionary change, because by making it second nature in your business for people to be constantly questioning, thinking creatively and looking for new solutions, they are more likely to stand a chance of finding something that is a genuine, step-change innovation.

Whichever strategy you choose to follow, it should focus on three main areas:

1. Product...

Creating new products, services or markets, or adapting existing ones to differentiate from competitors and increase value, or perceived value, from customers.

2. Process...

New ways of doing things, improve or replace business processes that increase efficiency, productivity or reliability, for example.

3. Organisation...

Finding new ways of structuring your teams or managing and leading people in creative ways.

Your strategy and focus should help change people's perceptions about their job and why they work for you or your company. It should engage them sufficiently so that they feel they are not coming to work just to earn money. The strategy must be clearly communicated through the company vision, so that your people understand where the business is going and feel inspired to not just be a passenger on the journey, but play an integral role in contributing to the end destination. That of course, requires excellent leadership – something we shall be looking at in a dedicated chapter later on – but fundamentally, I believe that if people really, really want to deliver ground-breaking products or services, they will. They will find a way. If they're not that bothered, they won't.

Which is why we're looking at people next.

1 *The British Standards Institution, August 2009*
2 *Seth Godin, Fast Company 2003*
3 *Logitech, Designed for the Digital Future, 2009 Annual Report*
4 *Jerry Garcia*

So, let's talk about people...

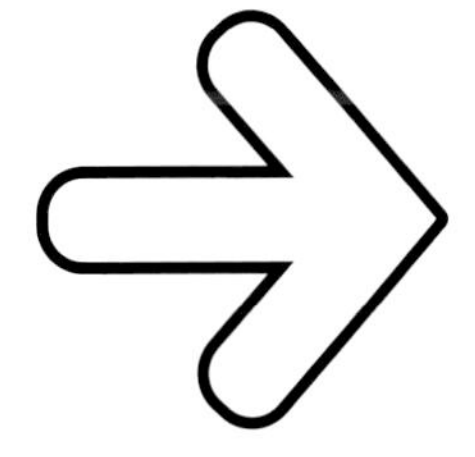

Peo ple...

As clichéd as it might sound, in my view innovation is delivered through the talent of your people: what they do and how they contribute to your organisation. *A question you might want to ask some of your colleagues:*

> "Is innovation part of your job?"

I'm going to suggest that most of them will say no. Of course we want to get to a position where the next time you ask them, they will say yes. But that change will take time and the starting point could be you or your executive team.

In my experience working with businesses, the change the business wants to instil in its people has to start at the top. Not enough senior executives recognise how much they can learn from all the people around them. Usually, top business teams are full of the same sort of people – it's of course a generalisation but why does it seem that so many of the world's biggest businesses are all run by middle-aged white guys? Sure they're run successfully but when board rooms are full of the same type of people, who share the same values, who followed similar career paths, isn't it likely – and now obvious – that they will all come up with the same ideas?

It's diverse teams that have a better chance of thinking differently because it's in their diversity that we find different viewpoints and different perspectives – the very things that help to stimulate fresh thinking and new answers. So as well as actively seeking out diverse opinions and input from all areas of the business, people who own or run organisations should actively seek out and recruit people who offer something different to the business, not just keep filling vacancies on the basis that Candidate A is chosen as the most likely to fit in.

Innovation is about people.

- How diverse (and I'm not talking ethnically necessarily) are the people in your business?
- When tackling pressing business issues, do you pull together project teams that always include staff who are neither directors nor managers?
- When was the last time you hired someone who was a little bit different, a bit of a maverick perhaps in terms of their thinking and approach?

The value of any brand is based on the talent of the people in the organisation. It's not a business that takes a revolutionary step or comes up with a must-have product, but the people behind the business.

The leaders of great groups love talent and know where to find it. They revel in the talent of others.

Warren Bennis & Patricia Ward Beiderman, Organising Genius 1997

Good leaders understand the importance of finding and cultivating talent. They recognise that one of their key purposes in the organisation is to ensure that they recruit the right talent to take the business forward. They're not frightened or threatened by other people's skills and abilities. So the first step is attracting talent. The second is knowing what to do with it.

When you hire people that are smarter than you are, you prove you are smarter than they are.

R. H. Grant

Many modern businesses still operate in a traditional way of promoting talent, i.e. the best sales person becomes the head of sales. But it's an approach that at best misplaces talent and at worst does serious damage to a business. Just because you're great at sales, doesn't necessarily mean you'll be great at managing a sales team. And whilst the person becoming head of sales has been rewarded with a pay rise and more responsibility, the business has lost its best sales person and, in cases where the management skills are lacking, contributed to a major downturn in the sales team's morale and performance.

> "To build something truly different you need to work in a truly different way."
>
> *Apple Website*

Understand and respect your people.

- How do you currently reward people in your business?
- How do you keep them motivated to continue being fantastic?
- How do you communicate the journey that they are on?

If you think of Apple you think of Steve Jobs. Of course you do. He's the guy who's always on TV. The one who appears on stage every year at the Annual Worldwide Developers Conference to announce the latest Apple innovation. So, isn't it surprising that Jonathan Ive, the man who designed the iPod and helped shape the original iMac and iBook, isn't running the company?

Actually no. Ive is a fantastic designer so that's exactly what he does – he runs the design team at Apple. It's the most obvious and most successful example I have found of ensuring that the right talent is retained in a business, so that people have the freedom and focus to excel at what they're good at.

So what can your business learn from the Apple model? According to Ive, nothing. Speaking at the Royal Geographical Society in 2008 he said forcefully and repeatedly that companies shouldn't spend their time trying to emulate Apple's success but instead should focus their efforts on defining their own clear, high-minded raison d'être and ensure that it drives the actions and decisions of every employee.

But in reality there is something we can all learn from Apple and it's articulated by Jobs below.

There's an old Wayne Gretzky quote that I love. 'I skate to where the puck is going to be, not where it has been.' And we've always tried to do that at Apple. Since the very, very beginning. And we always will. ”

Steve Jobs, January 2007

Cultivate great talent.

- How will you increase the experience and knowledge of your people in order to increase performance?
- When was the last time you asked your people what they want or need in order to push themselves and your company forward?
- How can you link the company's goals with those of your people in order to engage them?

The fundamental building block of innovation is creating the right network of people from the start who are clear about the company's goals and their role in delivering those. Without that it becomes virtually impossible to create the right conditions for an innovative and creative community to thrive.

A community spirit needs to be fostered. It's something lots of people want, but few are willing to risk being the instigator to generate.

- How will you promote collaborative working that brings together different people with different perspectives from different teams to tackle business problems?
- How will you generate channels of communication so everyone gets to share information?
- How will you foster a desire in your staff to seek out opportunities to help others in the business?

Creating the right community is a vital step on the road to innovation. However, it is a stage that takes time and effort to bear fruit. In order to give yourself the best chance of success there are three important facts to remember:

1. *You can't do it on your own.*
2. *You need to embrace change.*
3. *You should adopt the Kaizen approach.*

You can't do it on your own. You need to choose people in your business who can push the agenda for change and the organisation along the road to innovation. I believe that nearly all initiatives that are solely driven from the top are more or less bound to fail because they rarely excite or engage the very people they are meant for. They have a tendency to be seen as just another management initiative – something to pay lip service to before the next one comes along.

So the first thing that is vital to recognise is that the success of creating the right community lies in the managing director, board team and head of HR choosing the right champions to help them. These are people everyone in the business can connect with. This is a group of people representing all corners of the business, not just filtering and supporting messages from the top down, but feeding the voice of the organisation out from the centre.

The traditional business model sees management at the top directing the staff. It is in essence a monologue, not a dialogue. There are of course more enlightened companies that actively seek the input of staff so that communication becomes more of a two-way process. But what I'm talking about is going beyond a dialogue and establishing a company-wide conversation. This moves away from the model of management talking to staff and vice versa. It becomes a company where all staff talk to each other. This has huge benefits, not least of which is the fact that management will not have to intervene as often. Why? Because through a company-wide conversation - where people across the organisation talk and work together - many of the issues for the business that directly affect people's work, roles and responsibilities will be resolved without the need to involve the business leaders.

The second fundamental point is to embrace change. Innovation will only thrive in a community where anyone from anywhere in the organisation can voice an idea and, if it's an interesting one, can obtain fast and easy access to capital, talents and expertise to push it forward. *This may need a bit of a rethink on the organisational chart and...*

“Way of doing things around here.”

After all, it is unusual for businesses or organisations to operate in such a manner. Yet by embracing such a change from the top and giving people the confidence to come forward, you will create an open market for ideas that will ultimately benefit your business and increase the personal and job satisfaction of your employees.

Finally, adopt the Kaizen approach. This is synonymous with Toyota and is the best starting point to embed a move towards a new organisational community through incremental change in today's fast paced world. Kaizen is all about delegating, expecting mistakes and rewarding initiative. As a consequence, though it sounds – and is – simple, it is very difficult for many businesses to embrace. Traditionally, businesses operate on the basis of playing it safe and minimising risk. A Kaizen approach to business changes that, but in such a way that makes the changes incremental, palatable and sustainable.

The Toyota Motor Corporation employs well over 300,000 people worldwide. It generates more than 2 million ideas a year from its staff because of its bottom-up approach. Around 95% of the workforce contributes ideas. Imagine if that percentage of your workforce did the same. You might be happy with half of that figure, but whether you got a contribution rate of 10%, 30% or 95%, just think of the possibilities those brand new ideas could mean for your business?

Getting contributions, and it could be just something as simple as a suggestion box, means that employees care enough about their job, their colleagues and the company they work for to suggest ideas to make things faster, more effective or cost less. It means you're on the way to creating the community you need for innovation to thrive.

A company's competitiveness increases when its employees have a chance to develop and improve. There is a phrase we have always had at Toyota that says: "build quality in at each work process." When each of our employees strives to do that, the result is high-quality cars. So, I believe that the basic principle of management is to think together and develop together with employees so we truly build quality into each stage of our work. I have been with Toyota for just 25 years, which is short for a person taking up my position. But even during that time, I am thankful for the numerous opportunities to learn and to receive support from many people in many ways. "

Akio Toyoda, President,
Toyota Motor Corporation, 25 June 2009

Toyota has been one of the most successful car manufacturers ever. It continues innovating whilst operating currently in one of the toughest markets we have ever seen.[1] As well as inventing the 'lean manufacturing' system (also known as Just in Time Manufacturing), it is Toyota's adoption of the Kaizen approach to generate bottom-up change and innovation that is the main driver behind the company's culture.

It is a culture that has successfully embedded a supportive community across the business from the board room to the production line. Cumulatively, every day therefore, Toyota knows a little more, and does things a little better, than it did the day before.

When continual, small improvements are aligned they generate large results.

- How much experimenting is going on in your organisation today?
- How often are people exploring and generating new ideas?
- How will you capture and implement the ideas your people have to improve their own workplace?

Some of the businesses I work with already have a strong opinion that they're actually pretty good at what they do. Sometimes they're right; sometimes it's an opinion that on deeper investigation simply doesn't hold up. But even those that are at the forefront of their market and are successful, if they truly believe that they're already good enough not to bother with implementing a programme of incremental change to become even better, then it's not just their closed minds that I'm worried about.

It's what's going to happen when their competitors adopt a forward-thinking approach and are soon more profitable and more customer focused, generating improvements in products, in quality, in customer service that leaves the close minded, previously successful market leader losing customers and money hand over fist.

Whatever stage your business is at, don't see the status quo as something to be proud of or as something that is fixed and can't be changed. You've got to keep moving, because if you travel the road to innovation and at some point decide to stop, there could be a hungrier, more focused, more flexible competitor who shoots right passed you whilst you're admiring your handiwork.

So, part of creating the right sense of community in which the chances of breakthrough changes and innovations can thrive, requires you to embrace change. It doesn't have to be massive upheavals, constant re-organisations or a harsh hiring and firing policy. Sometimes of course it's inevitable that major action needs to be taken. But by focusing on more subtle, ongoing changes through continuous improvement, you create far more empowered teams and far less risk for your organisation.

In many organisations, such incremental changes are happening anyway. Week in, week out, people in your business are making suggestions, changing the way they work on a daily basis and questioning whether a certain process or system can be improved. This is all happening without necessarily being under the banner of a change or continuous improvement programme.

Why? Because the employee cares enough to be bothered!

Choose your innovation champions.

- How will you choose your innovation champion or champions?
- How can you use 'innovation' as a catalyst for change in order to help your people create a community?
- How will you empower your innovation champion/s in order that they are able to help create a community of continuous improvers?

The business benefits from becoming more efficient, more profitable or reducing its costs. The employee benefits from going home and feeling that they have made a valuable contribution. All this takes place without the business really having a proper strategy in place to direct and mould it.

So imagine what could happen if you delivered a strategy in which everyone in your business does it, thus creating a sustainable community of continuous improvers. And one of the key factors that will deliver that community is rethinking your working environment.

1 *Toyota reported a net loss of $4.5 billion in its 2009 financial year, Financial Summary FY2009, Toyota Motor Corporation*

So, let's talk about environment...

Envir
onm
ent...

So let's talk about something you can control, your working environment...

I'm going to stick my head on the block a little bit here and suggest that when nine out of ten readers of this book want to find a place for themselves or their teams to go and be creative, have a planning or strategy meeting, or conduct a brain storming session, the location they will choose for that activity will invariably be a bland meeting or board room onsite, or perhaps a bigger - but just as bland - meeting room in a local hotel or conference centre.

What this demonstrates is that when it comes to doing something really important that will have a significant influence on your business, there is nowhere in the current workplace that can inspire people to go beyond the obvious, to think differently, to come up with new ideas.

Worrying, isn't it?

Because if you can't feel inspired in your workplace to do something really special, imagine how uninspired your staff feel doing the day-to-day.

The good news is, you're not alone. Uninspiring workplaces are still the norm. Despite all the books. Despite all the great examples. Despite all the places you yourself may have visited and thought 'wow'. You come back to the same old offices, the same old furniture and the same old traditional layouts.

> Cultivate great talent by creating great places to work and eliminating cubicle slavery.
>
> *Tom Peters*

Let's be honest, who on earth would you want to work here? Luckily, there aren't that many companies that still operate to this level of...

"Cubicle Slavery."

But there are plenty of companies that still view the office plan as the chance to see how many people can be accommodated, how the managerial hierarchy is determined on size of office and the MD always has a corner suite, or where whole teams of complementary disciplines can all be located together – sales near marketing, accounts near purchasing, and so on.

So if you are expecting to inspire your people to think more creatively, to come up with new ideas and to solve existing challenges with innovative solutions, you need to give them the time and space to do so. Moving away from the traditional office environment is therefore critical in order to move away from traditional office thinking.

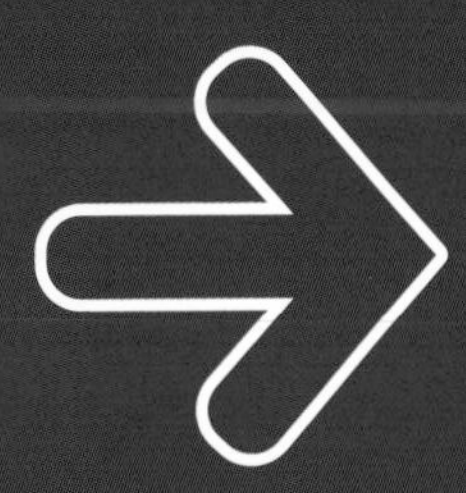

The workplace environment has a dramatic impact on how people work.

- How much visual stimulus is there in your building and how easy is it for people to write on walls or hang things up?
- Where do people in your organisation go when they want to think?
- How often are your people exposed to different perspectives, to outsiders and to sources of fresh insight to build an exciting and creative environment?

It's important to get the environment right from the moment people enter the building. Take the reception area below as an example.

Let's start with the positives. She's smiling! We've all been to places where even that doesn't happen. There are some flowers on display. Erm, I'm struggling now. What does this reception say about the company? We're an organisation that thinks and does things a little differently? We're a business at the cutting edge of our market? We value our employees and invest money in creating the right environment that gets the best out of them? We're glad you're visiting and we think you're going to be inspired by what we do and how we do it?

Nope – I don't think so either. And so it comes as no surprise when a rather dull and uninspiring reception leads to.....yep, a rather dull and uninspiring office.

This company have at least spent some time and effort in getting ergonomic seating and desking, but why does everything need to be grey?

"Image kindly (and a little embarrassingly) used with permission by TravelPod.com - who tell us that they have since fixed their boring wall problem!"

Imagine the difference if they just did this?

A change such as this goes to show that improving the environment to make it more inspirational, more conducive to creative thinking, more likely to generate the right culture for innovation to thrive, doesn't have to be expensive, avant-garde or just plain wacky.

Finally, how many of these have you sat in?

A typical board or meeting room. The irony being that it is in rooms such as this where people are expected to be at their most creative and forward thinking, where the inevitable brainstorming sessions take place. Are you feeling inspired yet? No...perhaps we should rename spaces like these as the Bored Room.

So, what have we learnt? Physical space matters. Make it grey, linear and boring and it will negatively influence the way people think and the way they feel. Make the environment colourful, organic and playful and it becomes far easier for people to naturally feel more productive, more creative and happier at work.

And creating the right environment doesn't have to be expensive, doesn't mean you have to move to a converted barn in rural Dorset or a converted warehouse in central London. The right environment can be created simply, easily and cost-effectively.

Just like this...

> "An office revolution is being driven by demand for new ways of working and using space. eOffice is a striking example of how space is being used by vibrant start up companies."

British Council for Offices Awards 2007

eOffice is a serviced office company with four locations currently in the UK. Here we see a small office (overleaf), a meeting room and an open plan hot-desk area (above). There's nothing here that you couldn't replicate with a trip to your local IKEA. So it's less about spending a fortune on the structure of the building and more about spending a little on the right things that make a big difference.

eOffice of course HAVE to make an effort. They are selling office space after all.

- What would you change if you had to 'sell' your office to your employees every day to make sure they turned up?
- What would you do to your current workplace to inspire and motivate your people?
- How would you engage and involve people in improving their existing workspaces?

Not surprisingly Google have got it absolutely right. Of course, they have hundreds of thousands, if not millions of dollars, pounds and other currencies to throw at their various worldwide locations.

The reception area says far more about the company's attitude and how it values its people than any corporate brochure or mission statement. The chill out pods, breakout thinking rooms and creative thinking spaces give people a great place to work that inspires and motivates them to fulfil their potential and exceed the company's objectives.

Terrace

Do what Google do.

- Are there other environments or locations away from your office where, from time to time, people could work?
- How can you create different spaces in your building for people to work?
- Does your workplace say 'we're an amazing company to work with' to your customers?

But if you're starting from scratch, why not start with that tired old...

"Bored Room?"

Take some design tips from eOffice, focus on a frequently used meeting room and use it as a statement of intent. It's vital that you make these changes slowly. Employees don't like radical change or massive upheaval. Whilst such action can be undertaken for the best of intentions, it often has the opposite rather than the desired effect. You could start breaking down barriers by simply redecorating. Not just in one room, but throughout the office. If people begin to slowly see that their office is changing, they will start to see things differently and start to think differently, more creatively.

Remember, you're reading this book because you want something different, so you have to do something different. In order to do something different you have to think different. In order to think different, you need to be somewhere different – intellectually and physically. And whilst it's unlikely you can relocate the office just like that, you can change your environment easily and without spending a fortune.

So doing things in different places, in different ways, with different tools in a different environment will contribute to increasing within your organisation one of the key drivers on the road to innovation: creativity.

So, let's talk about creativity...

Cre ativ ity...

Argh! Creativity! I'll skip this chapter because I'm just not creative...

STOP!

Let's start with what creativity isn't. Let's dispel a few myths. Creativity isn't flowery. It's not just for people who wear trainers and jeans to work. It's not something that is exclusively the preserve of designers, advertising agencies or artists. Creativity is about thinking – that makes it relevant to every department and every person in every company – including yours.

So skip this chapter if you have a whole organisation of employees who don't think or who's current thinking processes and outputs don't need to be improved.

Dispelling these myths about creativity is crucial. They're not just wrong but for business, they're dangerous. They make us believe that we have no chance ever of being creative, or that creativity is completely irrelevant to the organisation and its people and can therefore be ignored. And by perpetuating these myths, it limits the ability of any organisation to progress, to drive forward, to differentiate and to truly innovate.

Myth #1 – *"I'm not creative" or "I don't need to be"*

The fact is that all the research and my experience shows that anyone has the ability to be creative in some way. Let's take the following as an example...

Imagine you have a tracker rate mortgage and the Bank of England starts to raise interest rates so your monthly payments go up. Now then, your monthly salary remains the same so with an increase in your costs, and a reduction in your available spending money, you need to come up with some new ideas to ensure you don't end up a little more overdrawn at the end of each month.

So you start with making a list: the essential bills you have to keep paying. After the mortgage there will be council tax, utilities, insurances, transport and food. All of these costs you can't just stop paying, but you can think more creatively about how to get the same for less. You might switch utility providers, use a comparison site to get a better deal on insurance, use the car less and either walk, cycle or take public transport and switch brands in the supermarket to save money. The point is, when faced with a challenge in everyday life, people always use a form of creative thinking to resolve it.

Still don't think anyone can be or doesn't need to be creative?

Myth #2 – *"Only money motivates people to be creative"*

Therefore the more you pay the more creativity you get? If only it were such a simple equation. When people are motivated believing that their decisions and actions directly relate to bonuses or performance-related payments, the reverse is often the case. They don't become more creative they become more risk averse. They don't think about what they could potentially achieve but are more focussed on protecting what they could possibly lose.

Take 'Who wants to be a millionaire?' as a case in point. After answering a number of questions, the contestant might decide that they don't want to risk losing the money they have accrued. The fact is they entered the competition with nothing and the format means they are guaranteed a certain prize level. So the contestant never loses.

But do they think, on having reached £150,000 and faced with a tricky question, I have a chance here to win £250,000 or I could lose £100,000? Invariably, it's the latter. This is where money generates a more risk averse, rather than entrepreneurial and creative nature. Because whatever option they choose they would be guaranteed to win at least £50,000.

Myth #3 – *"Tight deadlines and pressure induce creativity"*

What tight deadlines and pressure induce is the requirement to make a decision or undertake a course of action. That is something we can all accept. Making no decision is often the worst course of action. What they don't do in any way is ensure that decision is the most informed, the most enlightened or the most creative solution to meeting a particular challenge.

When faced with any challenge, the most important part of the solution to meeting it lies in understanding what the real problem is. When people are under pressure, time is a luxury they do not have. As a result they are unable to go through an incubation period which helps analyse the underlying causes and work through a number of possible scenarios and the likely outcomes of each. We've all heard it, we might have all even said it at one time, but the outcome of a lack of space, time and freedom is the dreaded "that'll do approach". In essence, it's an admission that we know we should be doing more, but what we have done is take a short-cut – sometimes any short-cut will do – in order to reach an endpoint. "That'll do" means we know it's not the best solution. And the likelihood is that at some point, the problem will be back because "that'll do" is anything but a final solution to an underlying issue.

When it comes to understanding what creativity is, you need to approach it with an open mind.

- How often are your people given the time to think creatively?
- What inspires creative thinking in your organisation now?
- How do you translate the passion people have in interests or activities out of the office and bring that into the workplace?

Once we've got our heads round the definition of what creativity is and is not, it's now we need to work on how to instil creative thinking in the people within your organisation. The first thing to realise is that it is likely to make many people uncomfortable. Thinking differently requires the removal of tunnel vision, of assumptions, of playing it safe. It's not the normal way many people have been conditioned to think.

Creative thinking techniques are therefore not designed to put new ideas into your head; they are designed to take these things out of your head. Once removed, you are more likely and able to push away from the well-trodden path and come up with genuinely different, new and creative answers to specific problems and challenges.

> If you always do what you've always done, you will always get what you always got.
>
> *Mark Twain, 1910*

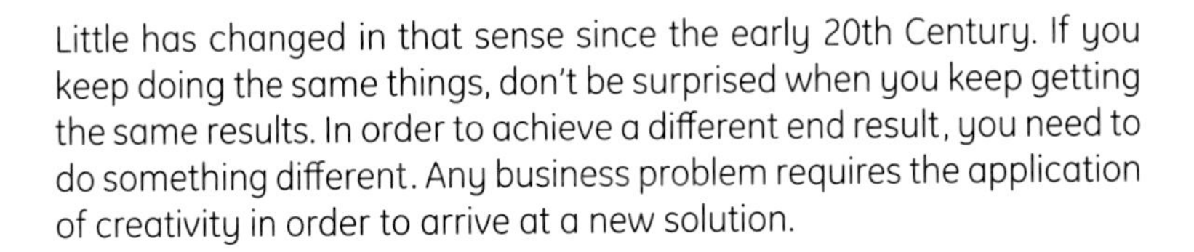

Little has changed in that sense since the early 20th Century. If you keep doing the same things, don't be surprised when you keep getting the same results. In order to achieve a different end result, you need to do something different. Any business problem requires the application of creativity in order to arrive at a new solution.

Take cost-cutting for example. You might think that is a straight-forward, non-creative task. But how are you going to reduce costs without compromising on product quality or damaging customer service? In mature markets, you need to differentiate your business from that of your competitors. If differentiation becomes a strategic business aim it will require the application of creativity in order to deliver it.

Another compelling reason for businesses to harness creative thinking is in order to keep pace with the changing needs of consumers and the changing nature of markets. In order to meet such challenges, new products and new services need to be developed, which require the application of creative thinking.

Every company needs to differentiate therefore every company needs to be creative.

- What differentiates you from your competitors today?
- What will you need to do to maintain or increase that differentiation in the future?
- How will you develop conversations within the organisation and with customers to gain the insight you need to develop new products or services?

I believe creativity can be boiled down to three main points: ability, aptitude and process.

Firstly, *creativity is an ability...*

therefore it can be learned. Imagine when you were little and saying...

I'll never be able to ride a bike. I'm just not one of those pedalling people. ”

Sounds ridiculous doesn't it? You're basically saying you're not going to even try and even if you did, you just wouldn't be very good at it.

Creativity for me is the ability not to generate something totally new out of nothing, but the ability to generate new ideas by combining, changing or reapplying existing ideas. It's the ability to use your imagination and to visualise the future. Therefore, it's not something you need instructions for.

The problem for many adults isn't the fact that they're not creative; it's the fact that from an early age the opportunity to use their creative thinking skills has been drummed out of them. In schools, colleges and workplaces across the globe, we're not taught or encouraged to seek out new things or to learn through experience. The majority of time we're taught it is better to take the safe path.

But surprisingly we're all born with the ability to think creatively. In 1968, George Land gave 1,600 5-year-olds a creativity test used by NASA to select innovative engineers and scientists. He then re-tested the same children at ages 10 and 15. When the children were 5, 98% registered genius level creativity. This had fallen to 30% at aged 10 and 12% at aged 15. The same test given to 280,000 adults placed their genius level creativity at only 2%.[1] The problem is that as adults, we're taught that there is often only one answer and as a result preconceptions start to creep into our viewpoint that restrict and limit our natural creative ability.

Whether you think that you can, or you think that you can't, you are usually right. ”

Henry Ford

Secondly, *creativity is an attitude...*

Therefore you decide if you are or if you are not. If you have the right attitude you are able to better accept change and the possibility of doing something new or different. You are likely to be more inclined to play, to explore, to be flexible and to always be wondering how something can be improved. It is an attitude that considers experimentation, repetition and trying things out to be the norm, not the unusual.

Finally, *creativity is a process...*

It therefore means there are tools available to help you become more creative. Creative people are continually looking at improving the ideas and solutions they come up with. They never feel a task or project is finished. By constantly revisiting their work and making gradual alterations and refinements to it, they make small, incremental improvements in order to push the product or service still further or make the solution even better.

The most creative businesses are the most customer-centric.

- When did you last have a proper conversation with your customers?
- How much resource do you spend on market research to gain a better insight into what your customers really need?
- How loudly and how often is the customer's voice heard in your organisation on a daily basis?

My purpose for this chapter is to ensure that anyone who reads it, particularly those having originally believed that they were not creative or do not need to be creative, is now coming to a different conclusion. Creativity isn't just a matter of natural talent. Like most things in life, there will be people who are better at it than you. But that doesn't mean you shouldn't employ it to the best of your ability. As a skill it can be learned and creativity is something everyone can and should be using.

Creativity for me goes beyond merely invention. It must be ideas that are more than just different. They must be ideas that are centred around doing something better for the customer. When an invention becomes an innovation, the tipping point for me is when it makes a difference and adds value – to a customer, to a business or to both. One of the main barriers to people using or developing their creative thinking skills at work is the fear of ridicule or of making a mistake.

But that is something that can be overcome when we look at and develop the right attitudes to risk.

1 *George Land and Beth Jarman, Breakpoint and Beyond: Mastering the Future Today, 1998*

So, let's talk about risk...

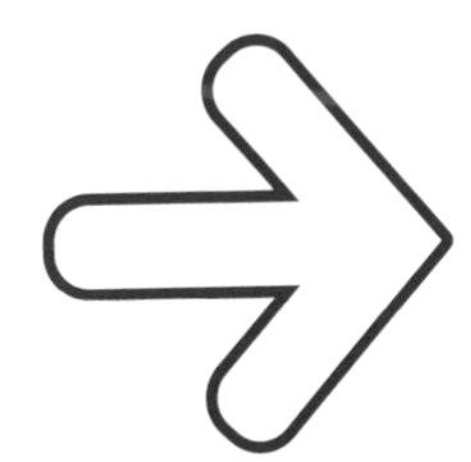

Risk...

Risk and innovation go hand in hand. But it's not cavalier-put-it-all-on-black risk I'm talking about. It's about balanced risk. Informed risk. I'm not a gambler and you might not be either, but I bet there are loads of similar things we wish we had invented or been the first to launch on the market.

Think of any innovation, any change, any new product or service launch and there will always be an element of risk. Even those that now seem so blindingly obvious and that went on to do so incredibly well, had an element of risk about them. Each time, someone somewhere came up with an idea, voiced that idea, gathered funding and resources to pursue that idea and ultimately turned an idea into something tangible and successful.

And that is often the first, and hardest, barrier to overcome: being brave enough to voice a new idea. Typically, we are only comfortable showing prototypes when they have been sufficiently developed to a stage where we're happy to do so. It's the same with ideas. We tend not to voice them if we don't think they will be accepted or even worse, if they will be open to ridicule. This attitude affects those delivering products or services. A recent report by the CBI[1] identified that attitudes to risk in central and local government would either stimulate or stifle innovation. A no-risk culture would ensure that services would stay pretty much as they are. The right attitude to risk that was managed and carefully considered would help deliver the necessary service or cost improvements that were being demanded centrally.

Let's all go back to school for a moment. The teacher has asked a question. No-one has put their hand up yet. You think you might have an answer but you're not 100% sure. So what do you do? Nine times out of ten, your hand – like mine – remained firmly down because you don't want to risk being wrong, being laughed at by your peers or, certainly in some schools I'm sure, more likely being the only one who is actually right!

Bring that right up to the present day, and in business many of us are still doing the same thing. Someone in a meeting has asked a question or raised an issue. We think we have the answer or a completely new way of approaching the problem. We look around the room. Everyone is looking at their notepad, looking blank or desperately trying not to make eye contact with the person chairing the meeting. So again, nine times out of ten, many people would keep their hands down, they wouldn't voice their idea.

The traditional business model is focused on minimising risk. Many organisations are inherently risk averse; they fear that things will simply not work – or not work out as planned – and therefore become...

"Expensive Mistakes"

Businesses will therefore look at everything from the point of view of mitigating, if not eliminating, all risk. But if this approach to minimise or eliminate risk means that you end up doing nothing, then you are assuming that the future will be no different from your present or past, and that you are happy with where you are today.

“Innovation requires risk but is the biggest gamble of all doing nothing?”

- Without becoming cavalier about risk, how do you ensure that new ideas are given sufficient latitude to push boundaries?
- Assuming that the world remains a rapidly changing place, have you quantified the risk of not changing or pursuing new ideas?
- As a business leader, what can you do to encourage more people to bring forward new ideas, to ‘put their hands up’?

In order to generate the right sense of community within an organisation in which the opportunity for innovation will flourish, it is vital that the business needs to accept failure as part of the learning process, and build adequate support structures in order to cope with it.

Business leaders, if they want to encourage creativity, need to ensure that everyone within the organisation feels comfortable suggesting new ideas and feels able and supported to push boundaries. It is also the responsibility of senior managers to ensure that the business has the capacity to survive if one of these risks goes wrong. This is what I mean by encouraging risk taking, but not in a cavalier way. For example, the business needs to plan to have sufficient reserves to cover any potential financial loss if one of the new ideas or new innovations simply doesn't deliver the turnover or profit expected.

Attitudes to risk are therefore an important part of leadership. In a research report undertaken by the National School of Government, it concluded that:

> **"In some organisations, there was a passionate belief in the value their products and services had for society as a whole. This encouraged people to think about what could go wrong and to spot opportunities to optimise success. Accountability for decision making at all levels in the organisation, with appropriate authority delegated from the top, was seen as a significant shift away from the 'blame culture'.[2]"**

The objective of the report was to better understand how high-performing organisations:

- Establish a supportive environment and culture for innovating and taking risk – while balancing the need to comply with ever more demanding corporate governance rules and guidelines.
- Motivate and incentivise appropriate behaviours.
- Learn from past experience and embed good practice.
- Deliver the goods.

The link between a company that strives for innovation and one that has a clear understanding of how risk management contributes to that is obvious. It is through strong leadership that the importance of innovation is communicated as a priority for the organisation and every single one of its people. By aligning its attitude to risk with its corporate values, organisations can move away from a traditional model of maintaining the status quo or defaulting to a position of blame for failure and move toward accepting and planning for mistakes as a natural, and expected part, of an innovative organisation.

Learning to anticipate, plan for and accept mistakes isn't going to be easy. In an interview in December 2006 the world renowned expert on creative thinking Edward de Bono highlighted that people are reluctant to be creative because they don't want to make what everyone will call a 'mistake'. He outlined that in his opinion the problem is that the English language does not have a word to describe creative ideas that just don't work except to call them mistakes. He said;

"A big deficiency in language, certainly the English language is that we don't have a word that says a fully justified venture which for reasons beyond your control did not succeed."

I found lots of words like mistake, aberration, gaffe, error, blunder, boo-boo, bungle but not one to describe this situation.

So, taking up de Bono's challenge, I created my own:

ju.ven.di.ceed

My definition of juvendiceed is...

> "A fully justified and considered venture which for reasons outside our control just didn't succeed."

This sums up for me what **'smart risk'** taking is all about. It's about investigating and working on ideas that are well-researched, that have been talked about with customers, that are based on a real customer insight and have full organisational support behind them. Rather than suddenly becoming cavalier, it can help organisations understand the importance of informed risk taking. If, over the course of the financial year, your business decides to progress with 10 new projects, only 6 may succeed so risk management comes into play when the business builds into its budget and expenditure forecast the possibility of 4 projects not delivering expectations.

“If you don’t risk anything, you risk even more.”[3]

- How would you characterise your organisation’s attitude to risk?
- How would you characterise your people’s attitudes to risk?
- Do the boundaries in your organisation allow informed risk taking or prevent it?

If you never push the boundaries you will never be able to reach what could be your own true potential or that of your business. Risk management isn't about limiting behaviour and saying no. It's about setting the right boundaries that you, your business and your people feel are there to be pushed. Another American writer, H. Jackson Brown Jr once said...

> "Don't be afraid to go out on a limb. That's where the fruit is."

In fact, there are many great quotes from Brown Jr that I could have used to get over the point that if you're never going to risk anything, you are never going to get the large rewards.

Risk taking doesn't mean taking radical or revolutionary leaps. It doesn't mean turning the company upside down, throwing out the rule book and ignoring all the little voices of caution in your head. It's just about opening up the business, and the minds of the people in it, to see what could be achieved. It's about ensuring that the business has sufficient contingency to cope with the expected juvendiceed that this new approach may bring.

I'm not suggesting businesses and organisations should take more risk just for the hell of it. I believe the crucial factor is that people need to understand risk – then they can make decisions and choices based on deeper customer insight, based on better competitor intelligence and based on a full understanding of the financial commitments required.

This won't eliminate risk, but it helps the leaders of businesses to weigh up whether the company's existing people and assets can deliver the new idea, whether any additional resources need to be brought in (and with it, the associated increase in costs) and how quickly that new idea needs to be brought to market.

Many of the existing books written today and speeches given by leading innovation consultants and thinkers talk about the need for radical innovation. But in my view, although radical innovation can be ultimately successful and beneficial, it carries a much greater exposure to risk. Radical innovation is likely to require greater resource invested over a shorter amount of time. For many organisations that is likely to mean that they need to put all their eggs – or just one huge egg – into one basket.

If we look at how 'serial' risk takers operate – Venture Capitalists – they don't invest all their money in one company or one idea. They spread their money around, hence mitigating their exposure. They invest a small proportion of their money in lots of companies, knowing that some will deliver them a good return and others will not. It's a risk strategy that is crying out to be followed.

The crucial factor is that by spreading the risk, the ones that do well will more than pay for the ones that do not, so ultimately it's a net gain. That's exactly what you need to be looking for in terms of your risk management. Invest in a number of new ideas and accept that not all of them will deliver what is expected. Consider each new idea a stepping stone so that the road to innovation is wide and solid, not the equivalent of walking a one-idea tightrope with no room for error.

Finally, as a business leader you need to understand that the majority of people in your business do not view their contribution in terms of the balance between risk and reward for the business. They view it on a personal level, on how they will be perceived by their colleagues and managers. It is therefore likely that this approach influences them to become less innovative and less creative, because they still have that hangover from their school days of not wanting to be the person putting their hand up in class and getting it wrong.

Bill Gates once said, "If you're successful in everything you do you have failed".

- How can you open up the minds of your people to anticipate, expect and encourage failure that can be analysed, learned from and ultimately benefit your long-term objectives?
- What can you do to increase customer insight and competitor intelligence in order for your people to take informed 'Smart Risks'?
- As a business leader how will you ensure that your business can absorb the odd 'Juvendiceed'?

Good leadership will overcome this, and many of the other challenges, on the road to innovation and so that is where we head next before you begin the first steps on your own journey.

1. *Excellence in service innovation. CBI/QinetiQ report on innovation in UK service sector businesses. July 2008*
2. *Innovation and risk management: a recipe for improving performance. January 2006. National School of Government*
3. *Erica Jong, novelist, poet, essayist*

So, let's talk about leadership...

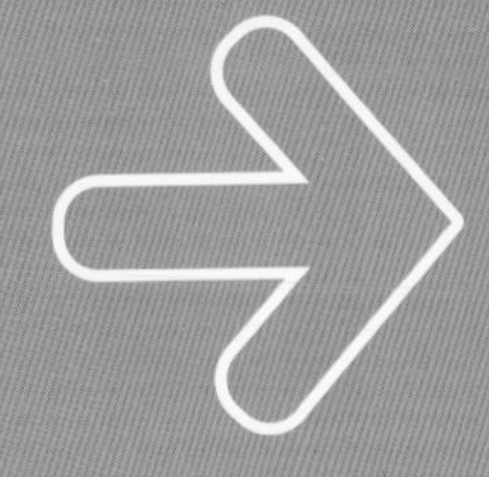

Lead ers hip...

As our business grows, it becomes increasingly necessary to delegate responsibility and to encourage men and women to exercise their initiative. This requires considerable tolerance. Those men and women, to whom we delegate authority and responsibility, if they are good people, are going to want to do their jobs in their own way.

Mistakes will be made. But if a person is essentially right, the mistakes he or she makes are not as serious in the long run as the mistakes management will make if it undertakes to tell those in authority exactly how they must do their jobs.

Management that is destructively critical when mistakes are made kills initiative. And it's essential that we have many people with initiative if we are to continue to grow.

William L. McKnight, 1948

William L. McKnight was a great business leader. If you're struggling to think whether you've heard of him or his organisation before, The Minnesota Mining and Manufacturing Company, you probably have. You just know it as most people do: 3M

3M is a global business synonymous with innovation. When most people think of 3M they think of Post-It notes (an innovation by accident as it happens), but it has been a company that has continuously innovated throughout its history. It was established in 1902 to mine minerals for grinding, but has obviously diversified substantially and done rather well. Sales in 2008 topped $25 billion.[1]

McKnight had what it takes when it came to leadership. He knew that attracting the right people to the right jobs was important. But that's only half the story. Once the right talent was in place he knew that leadership meant giving those people the freedom and flexibility not just to excel at their jobs, but by doing so, to inspire them to contribute more to the company than they were contractually obliged to do. Great leaders are great people managers. You need to understand how to manage people, relate to them and communicate with them at a high level before they will follow your lead.

Great leaders are inspired and inspiring.

- What or who inspires you?
- What or who inspires your people?
- How can you tap these seams of inspiration and galvanise the business?

3M created the concept of allowing employees to take time out of their working week to use for personal projects in the 1940s. Another company, Google, has more recently gained much press column inches and plaudits for 'pioneering' the same approach. Google engineers are given an 80:20 responsibility. 80% of their time must be spent on projects related to Google; 20% of their time can be spent to pursue personal interests in their work.[2]

When Larry Page and Sergey Brin founded Google in 1998, they identified that the company's mission was...

To organise the world's information and make it universally accessible and useful.[3] ”

They created a simple vision that drove every decision they made. What they also did was create a company vision – and ultimately a company – that people wanted to be part of, and still do.

Company visions don't have to be groundbreaking. But they do have to clearly communicate where the business is going, how it will get there, how worthwhile that journey will be, the benefits that everyone will reap and the belief that the organisation will become, or will continue to be, a great place to work.

As the leader in your business, it's crucial that you provide leadership that sets a clear vision that ensures a creative or innovative philosophy is communicated throughout the organisation and that gets the buy-in from every single person in the business.

“The culture of the empire comes down from the home of the emperor.”[4]

- What is your vision for your business?
- How will you communicate it throughout the organisation?
- How do you demonstrate you are living and breathing the vision?

Just as a company creates more opportunities for innovation through a change in mindset, leadership to create such an organisation requires a similar change. Traditionally, business leaders needed to focus on three things:

1. Control
2. Delivery
3. Profitability

In today's economies, the same business leaders also need to balance these against...

Creativity

Entrepreneurship

Risk

As a business leader you need to balance all 6 elements...

Control, Delivery, Profitability, Creativity, Entrepreneurship & Risk.

...if you are serious about becoming innovative and want to create the right conditions for your people and business to deliver that. Too much focus purely on control, delivery and profitability will inhibit the ability of your business and people to develop, to grow, to have the flexibility and freedom to think and do things differently. Your short-term business success may be secured with such an approach, but long-term the future will look far from rosy. Sales will plateau, competitors will catch up and overtake you and customers will go elsewhere.

Too much focus on creativity, entrepreneurship and risk may lead to catastrophic failure. But even if it generated stratospheric initial success, without the proper business foundations and focus, that success is unlikely to be sustainable and possibly not even profitable in the long-term. Getting the balance right is crucial. Innovative companies that are successful never forget the importance of balancing the foundations of the traditional business model (Control, Delivery, Profitability) with the flexibility of the innovative one (Creativity, Entrepreneurship, Risk).

The innovative business gives people the flexibility and opportunity to experiment.

- Review your current business plan – does it provide the flexibility to experiment?
- Does your business plan anticipate that not all experiments will work out as you expect?
- Have you built contingency into the business to be able to experiment and survive?

Have you ever stopped to think about why people you employ work for you? If everyone is only there because of the money, then you're going to have problems inspiring and motivating your workforce. Don't get me wrong, everyone wants to get paid for working. I know people who work for fantastic charities and do so because they have a real affinity for the particular cause. But they all want to get paid too. They're not THAT altruistic. They have mortgages, bills and want to do things in life outside of work, such as travel, that require cold hard cash. The difference here is that as long as they're not being underpaid, it doesn't matter if another charity or organisation offers them 10% more. Their salary is important but secondary to the fact that they genuinely want to work for their current employer and feel professionally and personally rewarded in doing so.

From an early age in life we're all conditioned to respond positively to rewards. That doesn't change as we grow up. It's just that the things that we value as rewards start to differ. Rewards do not have to be financial, though as I stated earlier, I'm not advocating you underpay staff below the market rate for their job. Rewards can simply be taking someone or a team out for lunch, or just a public form of recognition or respect for their efforts. It's important to strike the balance between extrinsic and intrinsic rewards; ensuring that there isn't a sole focus on promotions, salary increases and bonuses, but a business culture that rewards effort and excellence in different, non-monetary ways too.

When your staff have the mindset of my friends in the charity sector, then they too will primarily be working for you because they want to. They believe in you, in the company vision and they want to be part of the journey. They're not underpaid, but their salary becomes a secondary consideration. Because they work for a company where they enjoy the culture, where they are given the freedom and autonomy to do their job and where they feel suitably recognised and rewarded for their efforts.

"What's in it for me?"

- How many of your people are only there "for the money"?
- How often does your business go beyond the traditional reward methods?
- When people leave the business, are there any trends or reasons that keep coming up as key factors in that decision?

Don't be frightened by leadership. You don't have to do it all by yourself. You need to identify the people in your business who will help deliver your vision, who will help communicate that to everyone, who will help motivate people to be part of the journey. These are your innovation champions. It is likely they will not exclusively be your fellow directors or business owners. In your current organisation you and your fellow senior management team may all be viewed as...

THEM, not **US.**

I believe that innovation doesn't come from a homogenous group of senior executives or business leaders. It is likely that such a collection of people, whilst potentially highly skilled in the traditional business model, will not have the mix of diversity, energy, youth and hustle required to create and sustain an innovative company. Great leaders hire great talent, and then put that talent in the right job and give it the freedom to excel.

Your innovation champions need to encompass a broad spectrum of people across the organisation. A little seniority possibly, some middle management definitely, a lot of team leaders absolutely. Middle management and those who lead teams are more connected to the heart beat of your organisation. They are your communicators, they are your eyes and ears and they can instil a sense of community and common purpose that will never be generated by a purely top down approach. They have the ear of senior management but are also not too removed from staff, so they are not seen as THEM. Your team leaders can constantly reinforce your company vision and because they can interact with people from the top to the bottom, are perfectly placed to be the vehicle to push through cultural change. They can push this change both upwards and downwards, and by doing so make sure it spreads outwards through the whole organisation. But most crucially, as innovation champions, they can bring the diversity and different ways of thinking to any problem your business is facing that will ensure the approach to tackling it is both different and creative.

Choose your innovation champions.

- To whom will you give the responsibility to help generate a company-wide conversation and approach to innovation?
- How will you create the space and time for them to help deliver and communicate the company vision on a daily basis?
- How will you create an organisational community that connects with everyone in the business and the way they see the world?

Your key leadership challenge is to create the space and time in people's lives that generates the possibility for innovation to happen. We've already talked earlier in the book about the importance of community spirit. How it can make a significant difference in people's lives – turning...

"No-go, No hope"

areas into places people enjoy living and interacting together – and how the very same community spirit within an organisation can have just as powerful effect as it does socially. New, younger, more entrepreneurial companies I work with have a strong sense of this community or team bond. Conversely, I find that in more established businesses, the age and maturity of the business makes it difficult to maintain that community spirit. Things tend to slow down. Politics, procedures and agendas take hold and rather than a cohesive whole, the business becomes a collection of silos not helping, and some times actively hindering, the delivery of the corporate objectives.

Leading your business and people to create possibilities for innovation won't happen overnight. It will be a series of incremental changes based on inspiration, vision, experimentation, reward and change. It requires you, as the leader of the business, to recognise and plan for how to survive when some of the ideas you implement do not deliver what is expected of them. You need to step up to the mark and take your business and your people with you on a journey. They need to follow you, not because they have to, but because they want to. It's unlikely you'll be able to do everything yourself, so choose your lieutenants wisely. Look beyond the obvious for your innovation champions.

And finally, if you do nothing else to become a more effective leader, do this...

Ph.D. in Leadership. Short course. Make a short list of all the things done to you that you abhorred. Don't do them to others EVER! Make another list of things done to you that you loved. Do them to others ALWAYS!

Dee Hock,
Founder of VISA

1 *3M Facts, Year-end 2008. Sales worldwide $25.269 billion*
2 *Google Diversity and Inclusion; The Best Place to Work*
3 *Google, Corporate Information, Company Overview*
4 *Traditional Chinese proverb*

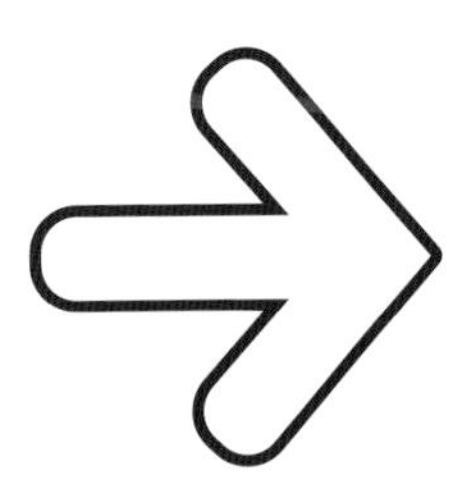

Con clus ion...

So there we have it. My take on innovation. A view that I think is more practical, more relevant and more beneficial to the majority of businesses and business leaders in this country than attending a workshop, going on a course or reading all the other books out there.

Because at the end of the day, what you need to do when reading a 600pp volume on innovation is attempt to distil it into the really useful, the really practical things that you can start doing in your organisation today.

And that, in a nutshell, is what this book does. It distils the really useful information about innovation that I believe will be highly beneficial to you, your business and your people.

I hope it has helped you to stop worrying about the end product or...

Doing something innovative. ”

You don't need to look for innovation. Look instead to change and improve everything you do. Look to inspire those around you and create the right environment in which the quality and frequency of ideas and insights can increase. Look to get the right balance between risk and reward. Because when you do all that, and the time is right, innovation will come looking for you.

With the economic downturn and recessionary pressures of 2009 leading many companies to divert greater focus to how to keep sales and profits up, I was recently asked out of the blue by a client...

My answer was immediately this...

Many companies only realise they need to...

when their competitors have launched better products or services, when the needs of their customers have changed and they are losing sales and market share, or when external and/or internal pressures mean that they need to quickly cut costs and boost profitability.

In those instances, for many companies, it might be already too late to start. The moment has passed. The time and investment required to reap the benefits of innovation cannot be given.

The good news – and the message I really want you to take away from this book today – is that starting to innovate before you need to start to innovate doesn't have to cost vast sums of money. You need to treat innovation as you would any other business discipline. The 7 steps I have identified on the road to innovation are very much inter-connected, and on each step I trust I have made it clear how taking those first steps involves small, incremental changes that do not require you to invest thousands of pounds or hundreds of man hours. But mine is not an exclusive approach – you may feel that your own organisation and people need to focus on just some of the key steps I have identified. Similarly, you may want to broaden my approach to include other steps specific to your own situation. The important thing is to remember that the journey needs to be all encompassing and consistent, so that it delivers the sustainable and organic benefits to you, your people and your business. Such an holistic, incremental approach to innovation should also mean you never get to that point where you suddenly find yourself surprised by competitors, by the marketplace, by your customers or by external events. You should never get to that dreadful realisation that you need to start innovating now because without expensive, sudden and radical change you're likely to be out of business in the very near future.

On the road to innovation it's the journey that generates the change and the added value, not the destination. In leisure travel they say that getting there is half the fun. In business, any organisation that sets off on the road to innovation with a clear strategy and an engaged and inspired workforce isn't just going to have half the fun, it's going to get all the huge benefits that travelling the right road brings.

So now you've finished reading, look to the horizon and take the next step on your road to innovation.

For your convenience the questions and tasks from each of the seven chapters, are listed on the following pages...

Strategy...

Treat innovation as if it were a business process just like all the others.

- What do you want innovation to achieve for your business?
- Who has overall responsibility for innovation in your organisation?
- Where are you now in terms of innovation and how will you reach your goal?

"You cannot be remarkable by following someone else who is remarkable."

- Identify your closest three competitors.
- What do you do that is clearly different to them now?
- How will you differentiate from them over the next 2, 3 or 4 years?

How well do you know your customers?

- How much information do you have about what your customers think and do now?
- How much analysis do you have on why they do it?
- How could your business satisfy these needs in newer, value added and more competitive ways?

Your strategy needs to go beyond competitor benchmarking.

- How can you improve your current top performing product or service?
- Who is going to be given the time, budget and responsibility to drive innovation, creative thinking and change?
- What will your competitors be doing in 5 years time?

"Don't strive to be considered the best of the best. You want to be considered the only ones who do what you do."

- Identify the products or services that you want to make obsolete in 12-24 months.
- Using customer insight, what new ideas could you turn into profitable products or services and launch within 12-24 months?
- How would you improve on your competitors' best selling products or services?

People...

Innovation is about people.

- How diverse (and I'm not talking ethnically necessarily) are the people in your business?
- When tackling pressing business issues, do you pull together project teams that always include staff who are neither directors nor managers?
- When was the last time you hired someone who was a little bit different, a bit of a maverick perhaps in terms of their thinking and approach?

Understand and respect your people.

- How do you currently reward people in your business?
- How do you keep them motivated to continue being fantastic?
- How do you communicate the journey that they are on?

Cultivate great talent.

- How will you increase the experience and knowledge of your people in order to increase performance?
- When was the last time you asked your people what they want or need in order to push themselves and your company forward?
- How can you link the company's goals with those of your people in order to engage them?

Community...

A community spirit needs to be fostered. It's something lots of people want, but few are willing to risk being the instigator to generate.

- How will you promote collaborative working that brings together different people with different perspectives from different teams to tackle business problems?
- How will you generate channels of communication so everyone gets to share information?
- How will you foster a desire in your staff to seek out opportunities to help others in the business?

When continual, small improvements are aligned they generate large results.

- How much experimenting is going on in your organisation today?
- How often are people exploring and generating new ideas?
- How will you capture and implement the ideas your people have to improve their own workplace?

Choose your innovation champions.

- How will you choose your innovation champion or champions?
- How can you use 'innovation' as a catalyst for change in order to help your people create a community?
- How will you empower your innovation champion/s in order that they are able to help create a community of continuous improvers?

Environment...

The workplace environment has a dramatic impact on how people work.

- How much visual stimulus is there in your building and how easy is it for people to write on walls or hang things up?
- Where do people in your organisation go when they want to think?
- How often are your people exposed to different perspectives, to outsiders and to sources of fresh insight to build an exciting and creative environment?

eOffice of course HAVE to make an effort. They are selling office space after all.

- What would you change if you had to 'sell' your office to your employees every day to make sure they turned up?
- What would you do to your workplace environment to inspire and motivate your people?
- How would you engage and involve people in improving their existing workspaces?

Do what Google do.

- Are there other environments or locations away from your office where, from time to time, people could work?
- How can you create different spaces in your building for people to work?
- Does your workplace say 'we're an amazing company to work with' to your customers?

Creativity...

When it comes to understanding what creativity is, you need to approach it with an open mind.

- How often are your people given the time to think creatively?
- What inspires creative thinking in your organisation now?
- How do you translate the passion people have in interests or activities out of the office and bring that into the workplace?

Every company needs to differentiate therefore every company needs to be creative.

- What differentiates you from your competitors today?
- What will you need to do to maintain or increase that differentiation in the future?
- How will you develop conversations within the organisation and with customers to gain the insight you need to develop new products or services?

The most creative businesses are the most customer-centric.

- When did you last have a proper conversation with your customers?
- How much resource do you spend on market research to gain a better insight into what your customers really need?
- How loudly and how often is the customer's voice heard in your organisation on a daily basis?

Risk...

"Innovation requires risk but is the biggest gamble of all doing nothing?"

- Without becoming cavalier about risk, how do you ensure that new ideas are given sufficient latitude to push boundaries?
- Assuming that the world remains a rapidly changing place, have you quantified the risk of not changing or pursuing new ideas?
- As a business leader, what can you do to encourage more people to bring forward new ideas, to 'put their hands up'?

"If you don't risk anything you risk even more."

- How would you characterise your organisation's attitude to risk?
- How would you characterise your people's attitudes to risk?
- Do the boundaries in your organisation allow informed risk taking or prevent it?

Bill Gates once said, "If you're successful in everything you do you have failed".

- How can you open up the minds of your people to anticipate, expect and encourage failure that can be analysed, learned from and ultimately benefit your long-term objectives?
- What can you do to increase customer insight and competitor intelligence in order for your people to take informed 'Smart Risks'?
- As a business leader how will you ensure that your business can absorb the odd 'Juvendiceed'?

Leadership...

Great leaders are inspired and inspiring.

- What or who inspires you?
- What or who inspires your people?
- How can you tap these seams of inspiration and galvanise the business?

"The culture of the empire comes down from the home of the emperor."

- What is your vision for your business?
- How will you communicate it throughout the organisation?
- How do you demonstrate you are living and breathing the vision?

The innovative business gives people the flexibility and opportunity to experiment.

- Review your current business plan – does it provide the flexibility to experiment?
- Does your business plan anticipate that not all experiments will work out as you expect?
- Have you built contingency into the business to be able to experiment and survive?

"What's in it for me?"

- How many of your people are only there "for the money"?
- How often does your business go beyond the traditional reward methods?
- When people leave the business, are there any trends or reasons that keep coming up as key factors in that decision?

Choose your innovation champions.

- To whom will you give the responsibility to help generate a company-wide conversation and approach to innovation?
- How will you create the space and time for them to help deliver and communicate the company vision on a daily basis?
- How will you create an organisational community that connects with everyone in the business and the way they see the world?

Acknowledgements...

For the majority of 2009 there have been a small army of people who have worked tirelessly in order to pull this book together. Everyone has contributed in different ways and for that they have our thanks.

Special thanks goes to the team at Let's Think Beyond Publishing (www.ltbpublishing.com) for their endless hours of designing, art working and on the majority of late nights, tea making! Thanks to Louan Hamilton for an excellent cover shot and the guys at Google, TravelPod and eOffice for their images.

For the many friends and clients who have read the numerous drafts and given me their valuable feedback, you've helped clarify some of my thoughts and contributed to delivering a tightly-focused work that is genuinely practical, useful and can be implemented by anyone in any organisation straight away. For a business book, that's an innovation we can all take pride in.

www.crisbeswick.com